# ICELAND

## *The Warm Country of the North*

# ICELAND

*The Warm Country of the North*

*Photos by Sigurgeir Sigurjónsson*
*Presented by Torfi H. Tulinius*

FORLAGIÐ

Original title:
ÍSLAND · *Landið hlýja í norðri*

Design and production:
*Elisabet Ann Cochran* and *Sigurgeir Sigurjónsson*
Photographer: *Sigurgeir Sigurjónsson*
Photograph assistant: *Helga Gísladóttir*
Layout: *Elisabet Ann Cochran*
English translation: *Robert Cook*
Film: *Fujichrome Velvia*
Paper: *Mediaprint mat 135 g*
Map of Iceland courtesy of Landmælingar Íslands
Special thanks to dr. Árni Einarsson

**Photography © Sigurgeir Sigurjónsson 1994**
**Text © Forlagið 1994**

Printed in Denmark.

*The following photos were originally taken for*
*Eimskip hf. 12, 19, 21, 24, 31, 32, 33, 34, 38,*
*39, 44, 46, 49, 54, 61, 65.*

First published 1994

ISBN 9979-53-242-4

**FORLAGIÐ** · Reykjavík · 2007

# Contents

# Torfi H. Tulinius - Six Icelandic Contrasts

## An Island, a World

A forgotten island in the middle of the Atlantic, sometimes even deleted in simplified maps, rarely mentioned in the media – unless some natural catastrophe or summit conference breaks through the barrier of silence which surrounds it – Iceland could disappear from the face of the earth without leaving any noticeable trace. One might even say that if it had never existed, the course of human history would not have been seriously affected. Nonetheless, this island is a world of its own, self-sufficient in many ways.

To begin with it is a large island, covering 103,000 square kilometers – as large as Ireland, slightly smaller than England. Alone in the middle of the Atlantic Ocean, it was formed from magma spewing from the entrails of the earth through the rift caused by the slow separation of the American and European continental plates.

Geographically, Iceland is not attached either to Europe or to America; it is unattached. Like our planet in the great expanse of space, Iceland – in the great expanse of the ocean – is a separate world emerging from the depths. A world within a world.

Similarly, Icelandic culture is both an island and a world. Like every culture it comes from somewhere else; transported here by the settlers who came from Norway at the end of the ninth century, it has constantly sought nourishment over the centuries from external sources, an island in the sea of cultures, drawing on the wide ocean of human creativity for ideas, models, artistic forms, concepts. Despite this openness, however, Icelandic culture is also a world apart, with its own peaks and valleys. In spite of its many contradictions, it forms a coherent whole.

Iceland, with its twenty million years of existence, is more than six times as old as man. However it is quite young, geologically, when it is compared with other lands. If the four and half billion years of the history of the earth were compressed into one year, Iceland would only make its appearance late in the evening of December 30th.

Nothing is stable in this infant among the lands of our planet. It is ceaselessly torn by bad weather, shaken by earthquakes, reconstituted by burning lava, crushed by glaciers, deformed by volcanic eruptions. Though changing and dynamic, and therefore always new, it stays the same and always will. Because of its climate, its location, and its nature, Iceland will always be in the process of formation, of trans-formation, its old parts carried away by the wind, the sea, the rain, and the ice, while new parts are created by volcanic action.

The same holds true for the Icelandic language, perhaps the most ancient language spoken in Europe: texts written 750 years ago are immediately understood by modern Ice-landers. The isolation of the country, the conservatism of its people, and above all a strong and rich literary tradition have assured that the language has remained basically un-changed through the centuries.

Modern inventions and concepts have of course necessitated the creation of a new vocabulary, but where the other Scandinavian languages have borrowed foreign words of Greek and Latin origin to form neologisms, Icelandic has enriched itself by making new words based on ancient native roots.

Like the country itself, which is renewed by fire issuing from the depths of the earth, the language of the Icelanders draws deeply from its past, remaining always new and always the same.

# Ungrateful and Generous

Whoever tries to cultivate a garden in Iceland gets to know the ingratitude of the land, caused not so much by the harshness of the soil as by the vicissitudes of the climate. Iceland is, in effect, at the very margin of the habitable part of the world, and could even be said to lie beyond it – the relative mildness of its temperature is the result of a warm current, the Gulf Stream, one of whose arms bathes the coasts of Iceland. Without it, Iceland would be uninhabitable.

A meager land with a fragile ecological system, Iceland has neither a rich soil for agriculture nor mineral resources. Yet it manages to offer its inhabitants one of the highest standards of living in the world, thanks to an abundant supply of energy and especially to its proximity to some of the world's richest fishing areas. Although it may not always have been so, Iceland today is a land which is very gracious to its inhabitants.

The Icelanders, however, have cultivated more than the land. Legends, poetry and tales from the past have supplied a fertile humus in which the inhabitants have been able to develop a way of life, their own traditions, and a flourishing culture, in spite of difficult conditions of survival. In this way they have been able to forge for themselves an Icelandic identity.

This culture is generous to whoever immerses himself in it. If it is to endure, however, it must be continually enriched. In a world more and more interconnected and homogenous, it may seem a thankless task to try to preserve a culture which only concerns a quarter of a million people. But, it must be strongly stated, it is not in vain to try. Much as this culture is vital for the Icelanders themselves, its strength, its fertility and its originality can enrich all human culture.

# A National and yet International Literature

In the twelfth and thirteenth centuries the Icelanders created a literature unlike any other at that time in Europe: the sagas. These are not epic poems, the fruit of a long oral tradition like the poems of Homer, but are in prose, and were composed by authors well aware of the literature of other Christian countries. These prose narratives constitute an important but little-known step in the direction of the peculiarly western form of narrative art, the novel, with their consummate structure, their realistic treatment of motivation, their restraint in describing emotions, and a delicious ambiguity which allows for multiple interpretations. Even today, readers of the sagas quarrel about how to understand various equivocal statements. The sagas represent, in short, an ancient art which is still able to stimulate the desire to understand.

Such a literature would not have been possible in isolation. It required a solid grounding in medieval culture. Paradoxically, it probably could not have come about without a certain isolation, or at least a sense of marginality. At the edge of the known world, without military or economic power, the small world of Icelanders had nothing but its literature with which to affirm its identity. Drawing on its traditions, its memories, and on everything which the contemporary culture could offer, it built up a literature expressive of both what it was and what it aspired to be, its way of thinking as well as its dreams, thus passing on a treasure of words, of situations, of enigmas which would become an inexhaustible source of inspiration for all of Iceland's later writers – and not only them, for since the eighteenth century the sagas have been known outside of Iceland and have inspired writers as different as Walter Scott, Ernest Hemingway and Jorge Luis Borges. Originating in the need of a particular group of people to express itself, the sagas have become a part of the literary heritage of the world.

# Force and Fragility

No matter how flourishing the economy and culture of Iceland may be, they are also fragile. Like the struggle for life, which is never-ending in this country on the edge of the habitable world, the economy is more vulnerable and subject to chance than that of most countries. This is because of its extreme reliance on fishing.

Having to count on only one type of product makes the economy very unstable. One can easily imagine an ecological catastrophe that would so seriously pollute the North Atlantic that no one would want to buy the fish anymore; national income would then decrease by seventy-five per cent, plunging the country into bankruptcy and its people into misery. Another possibility is a drop in temperature which would cause the ice-pack to block the northern ports winter after winter, and perhaps also those in the south, causing a progressive decline in living conditions.

The prosperity of the past fifty years has allowed the Icelanders to be somewhat forgetful of their precarious situation. In order to guard against possible hazards there is only one solution: to explore the possibilities offered by geothermal energy, the country's geographical location, and its cultural resources – possibilities which must be enriched and diversified in order to have a strong supply with which to resist the blows of fate.

Icelandic culture has developed out of a unique set of circumstances and it exists in an unstable equilibrium which can be maintained only through intensive creative activity. The isolation which impelled the Icelanders to construct a unique identity no longer exists. Now the world comes into every home – by satellite, fax, video cassette recorders – and there is a danger of drowning in the insipid chatter of the media. To avoid drowning, one must swim; to remain oneself, one must never stop changing.

# "Tender Indifference"

Island and world, constantly changing and yet always the same, ungrateful and generous, isolated and open, strong and fragile – Iceland is, like all countries, made up of contradictions. Although its landscapes are like no others in the world, as the photographs of Sigurgeir Sigurjónsson admirably demonstrate, its people are faced with the same challenges as everybody else: to preserve the past, to meet the present, to prepare for the future. Neither powerful nor rich, located outside of the main lines of communication and sheltered from war, their territory not coveted by foreign powers, the Icelandic people have had an opportunity to cultivate their own special features while adapting to the modern world.

The land has indeed its share of problems, but its low population, its homogeneity, its relative freedom from unemployment (*until recently*), as well as a reasonable stability in income, have contributed to a minimal level of violence in social relations and warm and direct human relationships. The photographs in this book show Icelanders at work and at leisure and testify to their easy-going and self-confident nature.

Life is good in Iceland. No doubt this arises from the good fortune its people have had in not getting involved in most of the great historical conflicts, but it also has to do with the nature of the country. There is the material comfort of houses heated by geo-thermal water, not to mention the voluptuousness of hot baths. There is also the beauty of the mountains, the sea, the everchanging skies. And, in relation to the landscape, there is above all the feeling that man has not left too much of a mark, the fact that one can forget oneself without getting lost – a country inhuman without being hostile, a country which allows us to understand what Camus meant by the *"tender indifference of the world."*

*For John and Helen Schettler,*
*we wish you were here.*

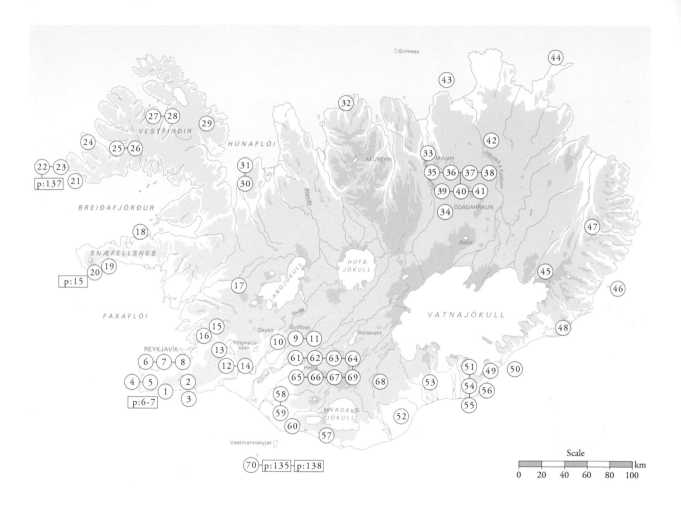

Grimsey

44

43

32

27 28

24 29

VESTFIRDIR

25 26

HÚNAFLÓI

31

22 23

21

p:137

30

BREIDAFJÖRDUR

18

SNÆFELLSNES

20 19

p:15

AKUREYRI

33 Mývatn

42

35 36 37 38

39 40 41

ÓDÁDAHRAUN

34

Jökulsá á Fjöllum

47

Askja

45

46

FAXAFLÓI

17

LANGJÖKULL

HOFS-
JÖKULL

VATNAJÖKULL

48

REYKJAVÍK

15

16

Geysir

Gullfoss

9 11

10

Pingvalla-
vatn

13

12 14

6 7 8

4 5

1

2

3

p:6-7

61 62 63 64

65 66 67 69

Hekla

68

Pjórsá

58

59

60

Vestmannaeyjar

70 p:135 p:138

Pórisvatn

53

51 49 50

54 56

55

52

MYRDALS-
JÖKULL

57

Scale

0  20  40  60  80  100  km

# Key to Map

**Photo number.**

1. Bláa lónið.
2. Krísuvík.
3. Krísuvík.
4. Sandgerði.
5. Sandgerði.
6. Reykjavík.
7. Reykjavík.
8. Reykjavík.
9. Gullfoss.
10. Strokkur.
11. Gullfoss.
12. Nesjavellir.
13. Þingvellir.
14. Þingvallavatn.
15. Laxá í Kjós.
16. Brynjudalsá.
17. Hraunfossar.
18. Stykkishólmur.
19. Arnarstapi.
20. Snæfellsjökull.
21. Rauðisandur.
22. Hvallátrar.
23. Hvallátrar.
24. Selárdalur.
25. Arnarfjörður.
26. Arnarfjörður.
27. Þernuvík.
28. Þernuvík.
29. Djúpavík.
30. Miðfjörður.
31. Miðfjörður.
32. Siglufjörður.
33. Goðafoss.
34. Skjálfandafljót.
35. Mývatn.
36. Mývatn.
37. Mývatn.
38. Mývatn.
39. Mývatn.
40. Mývatn.
41. Námaskarð.
42. Dettifoss.
43. Mánáreyjar.
44. Langanes.
45. Vatnajökull.
46. Djúpivogur.
47. Skriðdalur.
48. Hornafjörður.
49. Vatnajökull.
50. Jökulsárlón.
51. Morsárdalur.
52. Mýrdalssandur.
53. Öræfajökull.
54. Öræfajökull.
55. Skaftafell.
56. Öræfasveit.
57. Skógafoss.
58. Landeyjar.
59. Landeyjar.
60. Seljalandsfoss.
61. Landmannalaugar.
62. Landmannalaugar.
63. Reykjadalir.
64. Landmannalaugar.
65. Landmannalaugar.
66. Landmannalaugar.
67. Landmannalaugar.
68. Ófærufoss.
69. Þjórsárdalur.
70. Vestmannaeyjar.

**Page number.**

- p:6-7 Reykjanes.
- p:15 Snæfellsjökull.
- p:135 Vestmannaeyjar.
- p:137 Vestfirðir.
- p:138 Vestmannaeyjar.

1 Steam and ice, sensual pleasure and harshness, warm and soft human bodies amidst the cold and jagged lava fields. Surely no other place dramatizes the paradoxes of Iceland as effectively as Bláa lónið, the *"Blue Lagoon"*, a lake of geothermal brine, rich in silicon dioxide, filled by the run-off from a geothermal power station.

2  Steam, earth degraded by sulphuric acid and
   deposits of sulphur; at Krísuvík,
   only a half-hour by car from Reykjavík.

3  A ship stranded at the foot
   of the cliff at Krísuvík, on
   the south-west coast of Iceland.
   Working together against the
   hazards of nature is a prere-
   quisite for survival in this difficult and sparsely-populated
   land. Every village has voluntary
   rescue teams ready to act at any
   moment, with the co-operation
   of the Icelandic coast guard
   and the American military force.
   As a result of their common
   effort, the crew of this ship
   was rescued.

4  A proud fisherman carries a huge cod in his arms.
Cod catches generate 40%
of the total value of Icelandic fish exports.

5    Sandgerði, a fishing port on the Reykjanes
peninsula in the South-west. Capelin being
landed from a fishing boat to be rendered into guano.

6 The flamboyantly modern city hall, designed by architects Margrét Harðardóttir and Steve Christer and completed in 1992, occupies part of the lake in Reykjavík. Some of its rooms are under water. The elevation in the distance is Þingholt, on top of which can be seen the tower of a church built in memory of the great religious poet Hall-grímur Pétursson (*1614-1674*). This tower, visible from all points in Reykjavík, is one of the city's landmarks.

7  Swans, ducks and geese
on the lake in Reykjavík. To the left, by the side
of the lake, old residences made of wood
and painted in bright colors.

8 An inhabitant of the old quarter of Reykjavík, poet, novelist, translator, and polemicist, Þorgeir Þorgeirson is a well-known figure in Icelandic intellectual life.

9  With immense power, the Hvítá river plunges into a gorge with a depth reaching 70 meters, thus forming Gullfoss (*"Golden Waterfall"*), in the south of the country, two hours by car from Reykjavík. One of the jewels of the Icelandic landscape, this waterfall was rescued just in time, at the beginning of the century, from businessmen who wanted to build a hydro-electric plant.

10 The tip of its feather covering the pale winter sun, the geyser Strokkur seems to spout twice when the breeze carries the steam from its previous eruption off to the right. *"Geyser"* is one of the few Icelandic words to be adopted by the rest of the world. In Icelandic it is the name of the most famous of the country's geysers, now inactive.

11   Locked in ice,
Gullfoss is a wondrous world
of light and crystal.

12   Nesjavellir Power Station.
Water is heated by geothermal steam and
pumped to Reykjavík.

13 Þingvellir (*"Parliament fields"*) is historically one of the most important places in Iceland. In 930 it was chosen as the site for the national assembly which gathered once a year in June. Here laws were passed and lawsuits tried. Many of the major events of Icelandic history took place here, such as the conversion to Christianity in A.D. 1000, the allegiance to the kings of Norway in 1262 and the proclamation of the Republic of Iceland on June 17th 1944.

14 Lake Þingvallavatn, takes it name from the nearby Þingvellir (*"Parliament Fields"*). It is the island's largest natural lake, and is located at the edge of the central highlands. View from the south-western coast toward the highlands.

15   Mauve-colored and
sensual, the arctic river-beauty spreads along
the edge of a river.

16    Not only the flora,
but diligent fishermen as well cling to the sides
of salmon rivers.

17  A vast network of underground streams flows under the lava field at Hallmundarhraun, where the lava blocked the valley of the Hvítá River more than a thousand years ago. At the edge of the field the rivulets flow out into the open, forming the falls at Hraunfossar (*"Lava Falls"*) before emptying into the river.

18 Fishing town and administrative center of the peninsula of Snæfellsnes, in the west of the country, Stykkishólmur is situated on the southern side of Breiðafjörður (*"Wide Fjord"*), noted for its countless islands, where a myriad of birds make their nests, and for the abundance of shellfish in its waters. In the foreground is the ferry Baldur which carries passengers and cars across the fjord to the peninsula of the West Fjords.

19    Arnarstapi, a small fishing
village at the foot of the volcano Snæfellsjökull.
A column of black basalt lava
continues to resist the ocean's erosion.

20   Dazzling in its beauty,
and often thought to be the dwelling-place
of otherworld spirits,
Snæfellsjökull dominates its surroundings.

21 The broad shore at Rauðisandur ("*Red Sand*") on the north side of Breiðafjörður. Contrasting with the black basalt which dominates the area, the sand's color comes from sea-shells ground up by the ocean over the centuries.

22   Lighthouse-keeper and farmer,
Ásgeir Erlendsson, his dogs, his cats,
and a tame goose, enjoy the softness of the
summer sun together.

23    Ásgeir lives at the extremity of the
peninsula of the West Fjords. His farm, Látrar,
is the westernmost point of Iceland, and
therefore also of Europe.

24 Sunlight floods a flowery field and illuminates the quaint country church at Selárdalur, a valley in Arnar-fjörður in the peninsula of the West Fjords. Though Selár-dalur is now remote, many well-known Icelanders have lived here over the centuries. One of them was the priest and scholar Páll Björnsson (*1621-1706*). Despite his great learning, he believed in magic, and had five sorcerers burned at the stake.

25 Swiftly, swiftly flows the current
in these rapids of the Dynjandi
(*"Resounding"*) River in Arnarfjörður in the West Fjords.
The glaciers in the center of the
island and the snow which
covers the mountains for eight
months of the year constitute
reserves of water and energy
which far exceed the foreseeable
needs of the Icelanders.

26 Layers of basalt, formed by
successive flows of lava in the
Tertiary period, are character-
istic of areas outside of the
volcanically active zone.
Here the Dynjandi River
pours its veil of water over
the very beautiful waterfall
at Fjallfoss in Arnarfjörður.

27    Influenced by Konrad Lorenz,
the farmer Konráð, from Þernuvík in the
West Fjords, has revolutionized
the traditional way of raising eider-ducks.

28    Artificially incubated, the first
living thing the ducklings see
when they hatch is Konráð, who thus
becomes their *"mother"*.

29 Not long ago, Djúpavík in the West Fjords had a busy industry based on herring catches. When the herring disappeared from the nearby waters, the processing industry suffered. Abandoned in 1954, this plant has been gradually deteriorating from the weather.

30  In Iceland, sheep graze at liberty
in the summer. In September the farmers round
them up and herd them to pens specially constructed
for sorting them out.

31   The sheep are brought to the center
of the fold. Each farmer recognizes his own by
a distinctive earmark and leads them to one
of the pens in the fold.

32  The town of Siglufjörður in
    the north of Iceland. For a long
    time one of the main centers
    of the herring industry, the
    population decreased dramati-
    cally during the sixties with the
    disappearance of the herring.
    Owing to the proximity of
    fishing banks, however, Siglu-
    fjörður remains a busy port.

33   The waterfall at Goðafoss
(*"Cascade of the Gods"*). Legend has it that
pagan idols were flung down
here after the conversion to Christianity.

34    Organ-pipes of lava,
this striking columnar basalt constitutes
a true bas-relief in the gorges of the river
Skjálfandafljót.

35 One of the treasures of Iceland, Lake Mývatn on the edge of the desert Ódáðahraun (*"Lava-field of violent deeds"*). The pseudo-craters in the foreground were formed 2500 years ago when lava flowed into the lake. Steam which was trapped under the lava broke through it, creating these pustules which resemble, but are not, craters. In the left background is the mountain Námafjall, which gets its light color from high-temperature geothermal fields.

36   On the side of Lake Mývatn,
the farm Kálfaströnd, situated on a peninsula
formed by pseudo-craters.

37 Farm children at Grænavatn, in the Lake Mývatn area. Summer vacations from school are among the longest in Europe, lasting from the end of May to the beginning of September. Traditionally, farm children help the adults during this period, especially with the hay. Nowadays the work that was done by children is performed largely by machines.

38 Cows being led to pasture after milking. An idyllic scene on the shore of Lake Mývatn. The islands in the lake are pseudo-craters. The Mývatn area is a green oasis on the edge of the desert and, in addition to its beauty, boasts delicious trout and an important and extremely varied bird-life.

39   Handing down traditions,
the farmer Sigurveig Sigtryggsdóttir,
shows a little girl the old way
of spinning wool.

40    For centuries sheep were a
basic means of subsistence for Icelanders.
The milk and the meat gave food,
and the wool was used for garments.

41 This clay terrain near the sulphurous zone Námaskarð shows the effect of geothermal vapor on the soil. At the time of its eruption from the surface, hydrogen sulphide comes into contact with the oxygen of the atmosphere, forming sulphuric acid which transforms the basaltic soil, giving it a light color and a sticky consistency.

42 Said to be the most powerful waterfall in Europe, with a height of 44 meters and an average flow of 193 cubic meters a second, Dettifoss is located on the river Jökulsá á Fjöllum, which flows down from the largest glacier in Iceland and Europe, Vatna-jökull, and into the bay at Öxarfjörður in the North-east.

43   A colony of puffins
in the islands of Mánáreyjar
off the north coast.

44 A crowd of kittiwakes and a colony of gannets on the crag Karlinn (*"Old Fellow"*) off the peninsula of Langanes in the North-east. Gannets nest only in remote islands. Apart from the mating and nesting period, they spend their time at sea.

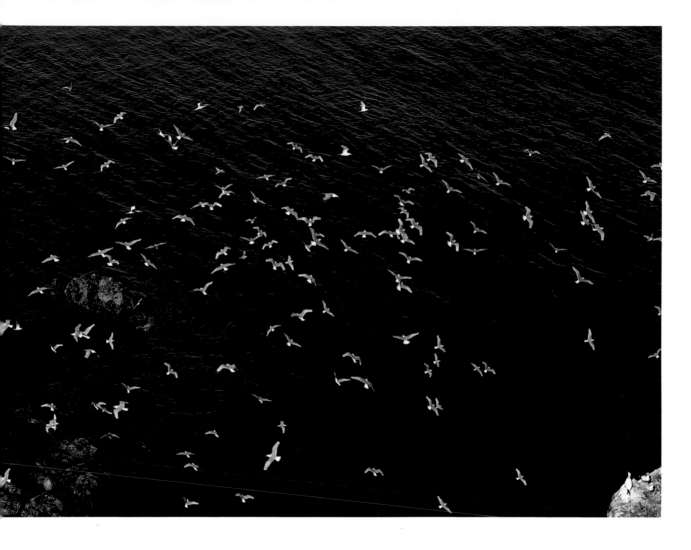

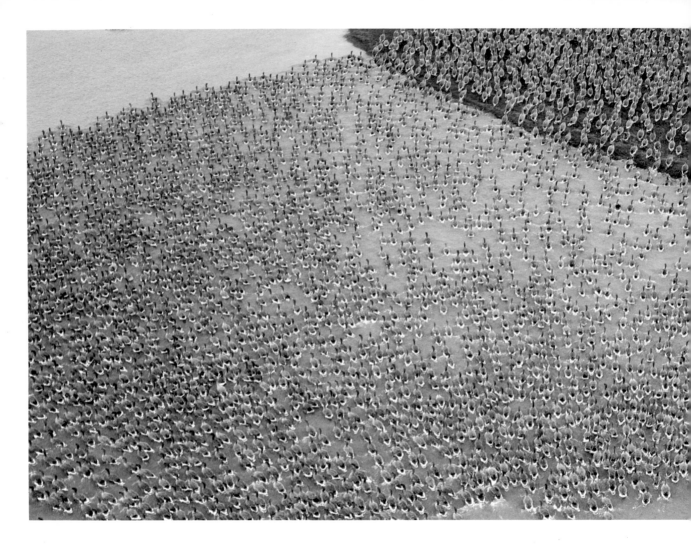

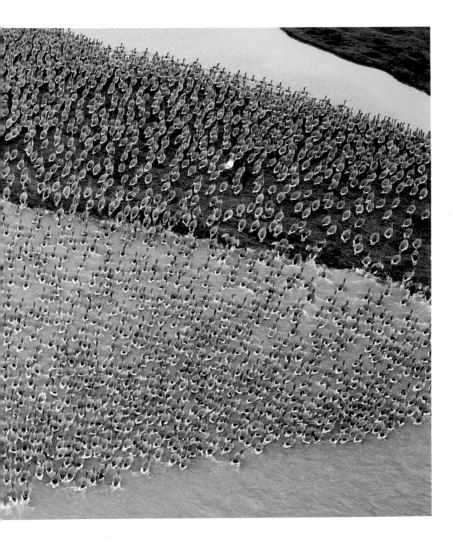

45 Unable to fly during the moulting season, the pink-footed goose spends this period in hard-to-reach areas, like these lakes surrounded by shifting sands on the northern edge of the Vatnajökull glacier.

46    Djúpivogur in the East Fjords is dominated by
the magnificent peak of Búlandstindur (*1069 m*),
carved by the Ice Age glacier into the basaltic
layers of the Tertiary period.

47  A gusty sky above the farm
Stóra-Sandfell, in the valley Skriðdalur in
the East Fjords.

48   A faithful companion from the time
of the first settlers, the Icelandic horse is
part of the landscape.

49  11,000 square kilometers of the
    surface of Iceland are covered
    with ice. Vatnajökull, the largest
    glacier, covers 8,400 square
    kilometers and is as much
    as a thousand meters thick.
    The amount of ice contained
    in this glacier alone is estimated
    at 3,300 cubic kilometers.
    The thickness forces tongues
    down into lower areas, making
    them fairly easy of access.
    A few steps can thus transport
    you to a fairy world.

50   Huge pieces of ice
in the lagoon Jökulsárlón, on the
southern edge of Vatnajökull.

51 Glaciers, with their immense
weight, crush and grind rocks.
Glacial tongues and rivers
convey the resulting mixture,
creating this mosaic surface
at the end of the valley of
Morsárdalur, south of Vatnajökull. In the foreground,
a clump of wild thyme has
taken root among the stones.

52   Clouds sculpted by the wind
above the plain of black basaltic
cinders at Mýrdalssandur
on the south coast.

53   Clouds tinted pink
by the setting sun. Below the clouds,
the cliff of Lómagnúpur (*688 m*)
and Öræfajökull.

54 The volcano Öræfajökull, 2,119 meters high and the highest peak in Iceland, forms the southern tip of Vatnajökull. Two eruptions are recorded since the settlement of Iceland, the first in 1362. A flood of sediment laid waste the surrounding area. Ten cubic kilometers of pumice-stone were ejected into the atmosphere. Previously one of the most fertile regions of the country, the area near the volcano then acquired the name Öræfasveit (*"Lifeless Region"*).

55 Svartifoss (*"Black Waterfall"*),
in the national park at Skaftafell, graces
a wall of columnar basalt.

56 A perfect rainbow crowning
the Öræfasveit region.
The sign in the foreground
points to a nearby landing-field.
Long separated from other
inhabited areas by raging rivers
flowing from Vatnajökull, the
isolation of Öræfasveit was
ended in 1974 with the building
of bridges. Until then the rivers
had to be forded – providing
they were not too deep.
Sometimes the sheep had to be
carried to the slaughter-houses
by airplane.

57  The waterfall Skógafoss (*60 m*), on the southern coast. Legend has it that the viking Þrasi, the first settler in this region, hid a treasure behind the fall. A few centuries ago, some bold adventurers set out to retrieve it, but in trying to pull the chest out the handle came loose, and the chest sank too deep into the mud to be recovered. The handle was supposedly used to decorate the door of a local church, and can be seen today in the museum at nearby Skógar.

58   Nudging it tenderly, the cow gives a warm
welcome to its new-born calf.

59    Placid yet curious, these young cows
study the photographer.

60 The waterfall Seljalandsfoss, at the foot of the glacier Eyjafjallajökull on the south coast, is approximately 60 meters high. A footpath leads behind the waterfall. In the distance one can see the alluvial plain of Markarfljótsaurar as well as the small farm of Hamragarðar with hay drying in the sun.

61 Climbing the mountain Bláhnúkur (*943 m*) in the rhyolitic region of Landmannalaugar in the Torfajökull range. A volcanic rock rich in silica, rhyolite is light in color when it is emitted from sub-glacial eruptions, but it is often tinted by iron oxides: blue and green by ferrous oxide, red and yellow by ferric oxide.

62 Magnificent panorama
from the peak of Bláhnúkur.
In the foreground, rhyolite
hills of the Torfajökull range,
with the lava field Lauga -
hraun which once flowed
toward the right of the photo.
To the rear, the peak of Mount
Hekla (*1,500 m*) dominates
the area.

63  The valleys of sulphurous
    gases, or Reykjadalir (*literally,*
    *"Valleys of Steam"*) in the Torfa-
    jökull range are more than 800
    meters above sea level. In spite
    of the geothermal activity, the
    snow never melts – but the steam
    carves it into some strange shapes.

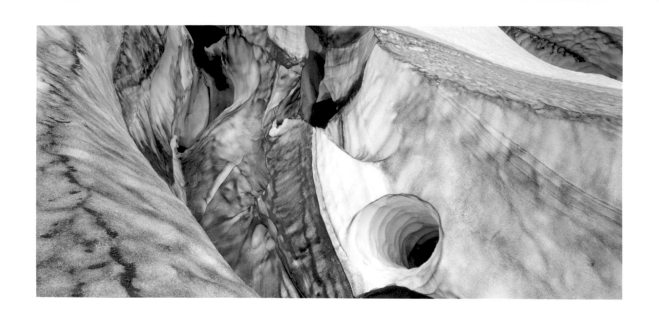

64   White, blue, gray.
Lines, circles, and curves.  Nature is a sculptor
with a strong sense of geometry.

65   The hot springs make possible a
delicate but tenacious vegetation composed of algae,
moss, and various kinds of higher plants.

66　Rhyolite, permanent snow and moss
in all shades of green constitute the unique beauty
of the Torfajökull area.

67 The valley of Jökulgil (*"Glacier Gorge"*), at the foot of the glacier Torfajökull which gives its name to the entire rhyolitic range in the southern part of the central desert. This region is also called Fjallabak (*"Back of the Mountains"*), because in the old days it was crossed by travellers who wanted to avoid fording the dangerous rivers on the southern coast.

68 The natural bridge over the
waterfall Ófærufoss, in the
volcanic fissure of Eldgjá to
the east of Landmannalaugar,
results from an alternation
of soft and hard layers of rock.
The water hollowed out the
soft rock which was under
a layer of hard rock, thus
creating this bridge, which
finally collapsed in the Spring
of 1993.

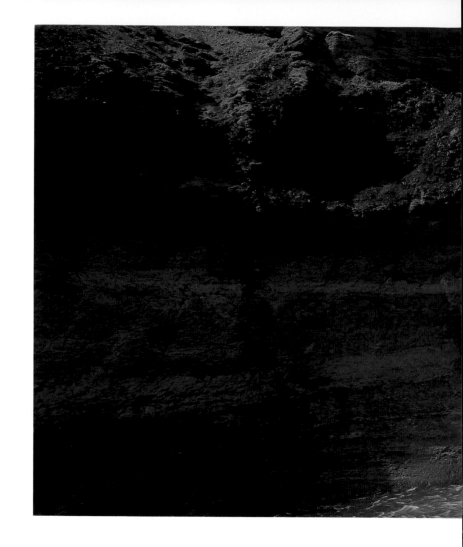

69 The waterfall Dynkur (*"Rumbling Noise"*) takes the form of a massive stairway, 38 meters high. It is part of the river Þjórsá, the longest river in Iceland, which originates at the glacier Hofsjökull in the center of the island and flows for 212 kilometers before entering the ocean on the southern coast.

70  A colony of gannets on the
island of Hellisey, one of the
Vestmann Islands which lie
just off the southern coast.
The Vestmann Islands are
volcanoes in the sea.
The most recent eruptions
took place in 1963, when the
island of Surtsey was created
by a submarine emission,
and in 1973, when a fissure
opened on Heimaey, the only
inhabited island in the group.
The 5,500 inhabitants had
to be evacuated overnight.

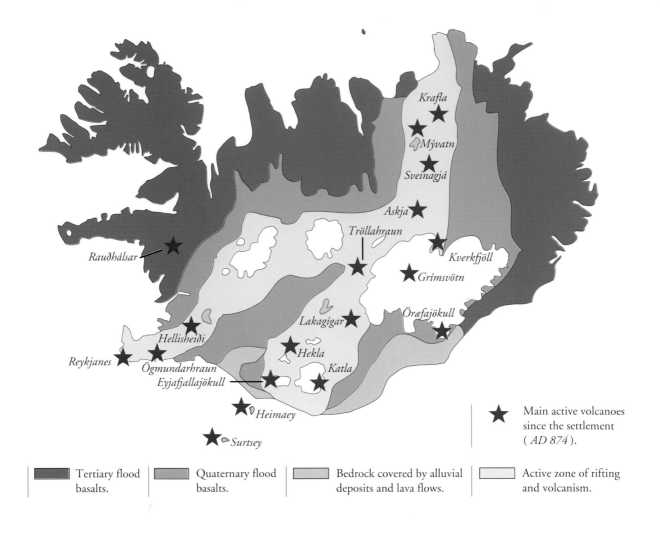

Krafla

Mývatn

Sveinagjá

Askja

Tröllahraun

Kverkfjöll

Grímsvötn

Rauðhálsar

Öræfajökull

Lakagígar

Hellisheiði

Hekla

Reykjanes

Katla

Ögmundarhraun

Eyjafjallajökull

Heimaey

Surtsey

★ Main active volcanoes since the settlement (*AD 874*).

Tertiary flood basalts.  Quaternary flood basalts.  Bedrock covered by alluvial deposits and lava flows.  Active zone of rifting and volcanism.

# Some facts about Iceland

## A Few Statistics

Iceland lies between 63 and 66 degrees north latitude, 287 kilometers from Greenland, 798 kilometers from Scotland and 970 kilometers from Norway. The North of the island just misses the Arctic Circle, which passes through the island of Grímsey off the north coast. The surface measurement of the island is 103,000 square kilometers, of which 11% are covered by glaciers, 10% by lava fields, 20% by land suitable for grazing, and only 1% by tilled soil.

The population in 1993 was 260,000, and the growth rate is 1.25% a year. Infant mortality is 0.6%, and life expectancy is 76 years for men, 80 for women, among the longest in the world. Reykjavík is the largest city; over half the population lives in or around it.

## Geology

The geological history of Iceland began in the Tertiary Period, about twenty million years ago. It developed out of what is called continental drift or the shifting of tectonic plates, a phenomenon which resulted from the separation of the earth's crust into continental plates which move very slowly (*a few centimeters a year*), separating from each other or colliding with each other or even sliding alongside each other. In the cases where two plates are separating, the earth's crust is replenished by magma which flows up from the depths to fill the gap. As a result, the bottom of the Atlantic Ocean is traversed by a chain of mountains called the Mid-Atlantic Ridge, which extends along the center of the rift. Iceland, along with the Republic of Djibouti, is the only place on earth where an oceanic rift occurs above sea level and is for this reason a perfect laboratory in which to study continental drift.

The rift crosses Iceland from the South-west to the North-east (*see the map*). It forms the island's active volcanic zone, which is bordered on both sides by earlier formations. Rocks that are at the same distance from the edge of the rift, though on opposite sides, have the same age, which is one of the proofs for continental drift.

Plate tectonics, however, are not the only cause of Icelandic volcanic activity. A few years ago a new theory came along to complement it in accounting for two phenomena which are peculiar to Iceland:

(1) *in the northern part of the country the rift makes a kind of loop toward the east,*
(2) *the volcanic zone divides into two forks in the south of the country.*

These phenomena, which puzzled scholars for a long time, have now been explained as follows: under Iceland there seems to be a rising flow of magma in the mantle which causes the earth's crust to rise. This is called a *"hot spot"* or *"mantle plume"*, and it could have caused Iceland's particularly active volcanoes. It also could explain why the rift tends to drift toward the east: it is trying to join up again with the hot spot, whose center is under the volcano Grímsvötn, south-west of Vatnajökull. This also would explain the division of the volcanic zone into two forks: the western fork is the older of the two and was formed when this region was closer to the hot spot. The eastern fork is more recent and corresponds to a shift that takes place when the rift comes nearer to the hot spot. This theory would explain why the most powerful earthquakes in Iceland have occurred in the southern coastal plain and in the area of Tjörnes in the North. These are the areas where the plates are subjected to the strongest opposing tensions, on account of the interaction of rift and hot spot.

## Erosion

Volcanic forces are not the only ones which shape the Icelandic landscape; there is also the erosive action of wind, rain, frost, ice and the ocean. Although there has always been erosion, it is the successive ice ages, beginning two and a half million years ago, which have made the major contribution to the present shape of the country. The glaciers did two things:

(1) *they hollowed out the fjords and carved the mountains in the West, the North, and the East;*

(2) *and they covered the volcanic zones, giving rise to the formation of kinds of volcanoes not known elsewhere.*

Ice acted as an inhibiting force on the flow of lava and the spread of ash, creating bizarre mountain forms; ash and lava were transformed by a sudden cooling of the magma, forming rocks called palagonite tuff, pillow lava, etc.

Erosion remains a very active force beneath the glaciers and along the coast, not to mention the threat which it poses for the soil. Wind erosion is at present one of the major ecological problems in Iceland, deforestation and overgrazing having in the course of centuries reduced by half the amount of soil which can support vegetation. This process continues, despite efforts to halt it.

## Geothermal Energy

Volcanic activity is accompanied by geothermal activity, because of the heating of water and rain which filter into the earth and come into contact with rock formations in the proximity of molten magma. In the process of heating up, the water expands and decreases in density and rises to the surface at a limited number of places, about 300 throughout the country.

It is customary to distinguish two types of geothermal sites, low temperature zones and high temperature zones. The low temperature zones are all located outside the area of

*The Heimaey eruption of 1973, In the night of January 23 a fissure opened on the outskirts of the town. The 5,500 inhabitants had to be evacuated immediately.*

active volcanic activity. There the water reaches less than 150°C at a depth of 1,000 meters. This water often remains underground for a long time, for centuries or even millennia, before rising to the surface, with a temperature between 50°C and 80°C.

The high temperature zones are located, without exception, in the volcanic areas, where the water reaches more than 180°C at a depth of 1,000 meters. The earth's crust is thinner in the volcanic areas and the magma exists at varying depths. The water is heated at a relatively shallow depth and rises most often in the form of steam, accompanied by carbonic gas and hydrogen sulfide. At the surface, the latter reacts chemically with the oxygen in the atmosphere, forming sulfuric acid which destroys the soil and leaves sulfur deposits.

From the fifteenth to nineteenth centuries the sulfur was collected and exported for use in making gunpowder. Apart from bathing and washing in hot springs, practiced almost from the beginning of human settlement in Iceland, this was for a long time the only practical use made of the geothermal resources. During this century, however, the Icelanders have learned to capitalize on this fabulous source of energy and now use it to heat their homes and swimming pools and to produce part of their electricity. Nearly 40% of the energy consumed in Iceland is of geothermal origin, and 85% of the buildings are heated in this way.

Greenhouse agriculture has developed due to the abundance of hot water. Although the results are good, it is unlikely it can compete with cheaper imported products.

## Climate

In spite of the northern location, which means that the sun never rises very high in the sky, the climate is mild and the temperatures are relatively high, especially near the ocean (*4.3°C annual average in Reykjavík*), thanks to the warming effect of an arm of the Gulf Stream. The average temperature in Reykjavík in January is -0.5°C, and in July it is 10.6°C. The average temperature is lower in the North and the interior, where there is also greater variability.

Located in the middle of the ocean, Iceland has little protection from meteorological disturbances and thus has a stormy climate with much precipitation. Warm and humid air masses, coming mostly from the south and blocked by the mountains in the center, cause greater precipitation in the South than in the North. This explains why all the large glaciers are in the southern portion of the country: the building up of glaciers depends on a balance between precipitation in winter and the melting of the snow, and major precipitation is necessary for this process.

As in many other countries, the climate is a favourite topic of conversation in Iceland, and in fact quite an interesting one because of its notorious sudden changes. The British soldiers who were stationed here during the Second World War used to say that if you weren't happy with the weather in Iceland, you only had to wait five minutes: it was bound to change.

*A baby fox treats himself to a meal of sea-gull.*

*A gannet raises itself from its nesting place.*

## Flora

Owing to the isolation of Iceland and the short space of time that has passed since the end of the Ice Age, the Icelandic flora consists of less than 500 different species of vascular plants, a small number when compared, for example, with the 2300 species in the British Isles. Trees are rare, taking up less than 1% of the space, and consisting mainly of birches and willows. The plants are for the most part those of Northern Europe, but a few American species have taken root. Trees grow at altitudes of up to 400 meters, and most plants up to 700 meters. There are also moss and various types of lichen, which are quick to grow on lava fields. One species, the Icelandic Lichen, is known for its medical properties.

## Mammals Living in the Wild

Because of the isolation of Iceland, it is not likely that any wild mammals lived there before the arrival of the first humans in the ninth century, except for the Arctic Fox, which probably came on ice floes. Mice and rats came along with man, while the reindeer, whitch live in a limited area north of the Vatnajökull glacier, were imported from Norway in the eighteenth century. The last mammal to arrive was the mink, which has lived in the wild in Iceland since the thirties, when mink-farming began and some of the animals escaped. Seals can frequently be spotted along the coast, especially the common seal or harbour seal, which is often seen in fjords and bays. Another species, the grey seal, is more likely to be seen in areas exposed to the open sea, like the tips of peninsulas. Whales are a less frequent sight, but are nevertheless quite numerous in Icelandic waters.

## Birds

More than 70 species of birds nest in Iceland, and more than 300 have been spotted. This comparatively low figure is made up for by the great numbers of individuals. The meager vegetation and the small number of insects result in relatively few passerines (*they comprise 17% of the birds in Iceland, as opposed to 60% worldwide*). On the other hand, there is an abundance of sea birds (*gulls, guillemots, puffins, arctic terns etc.*), of waders living in the marshes or along the rivers (*whimbrels, plovers, oyster-catchers, etc.*), of aquatic birds (*ducks, geese, swans, etc.*). Among the passerines we might mention the redwing and the raven, and among the birds of prey the gyrfalcon and the white-tailed eagle.

Due to the country's situation on the globe, birds appear from four different climatic and geographic zones: from the arctic and the temperate zones, as well as from Europe and America. This is a unique blend and makes Iceland an interesting place for bird-watchers. Moreover, quite a number of species pass through Iceland while migrating between Western Europe, Greenland and the northernmost part of America. They stay for a while in order to rest and feed before or after flying over the great Greenland ice-sheet.

## History

The history of Iceland began in the ninth century, with its discovery and its colonization by seafarers of Scandinavian origin, coming from Norway and from viking colonies in the British Isles. They brought with them their families, and probably also slaves, mostly of Celtic origin. The resulting group of people stayed outside of the developments in Europe for a long time, creating an atypical form of society; because of its isolation, the country was not subject to attack and no military force was formed which might have led to the formation of a central authority along royal lines. The country did, however, have its own political organization, in which the absence of an executive power was made up for by the establishment of a parliament, founded in 930 and called the *Alþingi*. This was composed of 39 goðar (*sing. goði – they were something like heads of clans, with both political and religious functions* ), who met annually to make laws and enforce justice.

This society without a state continued in spite of the conversion to Christianity in the year 1000 and the establishment of episcopal sees. It lasted until 1262, when the leading chiefs decided, after a period of internal struggle, to become vassals to the king of Norway and bring the country into his realm. Iceland remained Norwegian until 1397, when it, along with Norway, became part of the Danish realm.

The fourteenth and fifteenth centuries were characterized by the development of fishing and the export of fish, which brought some prosperity to the country, in spite of catastrophes like the plague which decimated the population at the beginning of the fifteenth century. Although under foreign domination, the country remained quite independent, the local aristocracy carrying out most governmental duties. The Catholic bishops grew in power during this period.

The Reformation was more or less imposed by the King of Denmark in the middle of the sixteenth century. The date usually pointed to is 1550, when the last Catholic bishop, Jón Arason, was executed. The Reformation ushered in a period in which Danish domination became more pronounced, the king imposing a harsher system of justice and declaring a monopoly on trade with Iceland. This monopoly impoverished the country, and a cooling of the climate which lasted until the end of the nineteenth century only made things worse. A series of natural catastrophes, culminating in the terrible eruption of Laki in 1783-4, capped the misery of the Icelanders. The volcanic dust, heavy in fluorine, which settled after this eruption poisoned grazing areas, killing a majority of the sheep and a good part of the cattle. This led to a famine, in which a third of the population died, bringing the number down to 35,000, probably the lowest since the first century of human habitation on the island.

In the nineteenth century a movement for independence began, fed partly by the discovery of the uniqueness and the richness of the medieval period, and partly by the wish to develop the economy by ending the Danish monopoly. This struggle, always peaceful, led to independence in 1918 and the proclamation of the Republic of Iceland in 1944.

The twentieth century has thus been marked by the gaining of independence and, thanks to the fishing industry, a phenomenal economic development which has made its people, so often afflicted by catastrophes and famines, one of the most prosperous in the world.

## Language

The Icelandic language is Scandinavian in origin and has remained so close to the language spoken in Scandinavia in the Middle Ages that an Icelander today can read Old Norwegian texts without difficulty, while the natives of that country are incapable of doing so. This is the result of the isolation of Iceland over the centuries, but also no doubt of the great medieval production of literary works which continue to be read today. To this must be added the desire – especially in the last two centuries – to preserve the language, which has made Icelanders refuse to import foreign words. Rather than adapting a word formed on a Greek or Latin root to express a phenomenon or a new concept (*e.g. democracy,*

*helicopter, etc.*), they prefer to form a new word using an Icelandic root, or even to revive an ancient Icelandic word which had fallen out of use. Thus the word for telephone, *sími,* is from an Icelandic word that meant *"cord"* long ago.

Icelandic is a complex language with an inflectional system based on four noun cases. It is difficult to learn, and yet an increasing number of people of non-Icelandic background are studying it.

## Economy

Iceland is prosperous, with a gross national product of 16,500 dollars per inhabitant, a low rate of unemployment and practically no inflation. At the moment it is going through a difficult period, due to smaller catches, fiercer international competition, and a serious foreign debt. What causes both the strength and the weakness of the Icelandic economy is its large reliance on fishing, which accounts for 75% of export revenues. This shows the importance of this sector, which has steadily developed and modernized during this century. Though only employing about 11% of the population, it is the driving force of the economy; recent decades witnessed a manifold increase in the catches, due partly to technological progress in fishing and partly to the extending of the territorial waters to 200 miles, which increased Iceland's share in the catches from off-shore waters. The present slump in catches, accompanied by unstable prices in the markets, underscores the precariousness of recent progress. Taking advantage of the energy potential of the country, efforts toward developing power-intensive industry have taken the form of setting up plants for producing aluminum, ferro-silicates and diatomite. Major investments in hydroelectric stations, however, have not succeeded in attracting hoped-for foreign capital, and the debts accumulated in financing the stations make up a large part of the foreign debt — 47.4% of the gross domestic product in 1990 — the servicing of the debt requiring the equivalent of 20.1% of export revenues. The country patiently awaits a resurgence in the world economy, but in the meantime the power stations are operating below capacity. A high-technology sector, focussing on fishing techniques, processing fish products and exploiting geo-thermal resources, gives hope for future growth.

The agricultural sector, based primarily on the raising of sheep and cattle, has been undergoing a thorough change in recent years, having been forced to adapt to progressive deregulation of the market, after decades of protectionism and subsidies. Meat and milk products supply the local market abundantly, and a significant production of vegetables, grown mostly in geothermally heated greenhouses, graces the dining-room tables of Icelandic homes.

Tourism has increased considerably in the past twenty years. Over 150,000 foreigners visited Iceland in 1993, and this sector is more and more important, both for the foreign currency which it brings and for the jobs it creates.

## Political organization

The Republic of Iceland, founded on June 17, 1944, is a parliamentary democracy. The parliament, or *Alþingi*, elected by universal suffrage for a period of four years, wields legislative power. The parliamentary majority (*as a rule a coalition rather than a single party* ) forms a government, headed by the prime minister, which wields executive power. The president of the Republic, whose period of office extends for four years but can be renewed, appoints the prime minister upon the completion of the elections, but is not otherwise involved in the affairs of government.

## The Rich Medieval Literature

The emergence of one of the richest and most remarkable literatures of the Middle Ages in an island on the extreme edge of Europe, populated by fewer than 100,000 inhabitants, has often been compared to a miracle. The literary production of the eleventh to fifteenth centuries can be divided into two main categories, prose and poetry.

*Poetry*

The earliest Icelandic poetry is preserved in manuscripts from the thirteenth centuries, but may go back to a period before the settling of the country and thus form part of the common heritage of the Nordic countries, in fact of all the Germanic peoples. This poetry is made up, in the first place, of the poems in the *Edda* and the other Eddaic poetry, poetry in epic form which describes episodes in the lives of the Nordic gods or the Germanic heroes, like Sigurður the slayer of Fáfnir, better known by his German name Siegfried.

There is also another body of poetry, the scaldic, which originated in the courts of Scandinavian sovereigns in the eighth and ninth centuries and which was very complex, employing a poetic language made up of circumlocutions and metaphors and requiring on the part of its audience a thorough knowledge of Nordic mythology. The Icelanders seem to have been the specialists in this genre of poetry, which was very much in favor in both the Norwegian and Danish courts in the twelfth and thirteenth centuries.

*Prose*

The prose literature began after the conversion to Christianity, with the first attempts toward writing in Icelandic. The first works in prose were religious, legal, genealogical and historical. A rich narrative tradition developed in the twelfth century with the composition of the sagas, which were prose tales on various subjects: lives of Icelandic bishops; lives of Scandinavian kings from the distant or not so distant past or even the present; contemporary chronicles of Icelandic life; and legendary tales of heroes of long ago.

The most noteworthy sagas are the Íslendinga-sögur, or *"Sagas of Icelanders,"* composed for the most part in the thirteenth century. These have as their main characters Icelanders who had lived two or three centuries earlier, around the year 1000, and the sagas tell of their conflicts in Iceland or their adventures abroad. These lively and readable narratives are characterized by a realistic description of social relations, a laconic style tinged with irony, a sense of the complexity of the causes and consequences of human actions, and a deep interest in human motivation, whether known or unknown. These sagas have much literary value and are far from having yielded up all their secrets.